C000136864

by Iain Gray

Lang**Syne**

PUBLISHING

WRITING *to* REMEMBER

Lang**Syne**

PUBLISHING

WRITING *to* REMEMBER

79 Main Street, Newtongrange,
Midlothian EH22 4NA
Tel: 0131 344 0414   Fax: 0845 075 6085
E-mail: info@lang-syne.co.uk
www.langsyneshop.co.uk

Design by Dorothy Meikle
Printed by Printwell Ltd
© Lang Syne Publishers Ltd 2019

ISBN 978-1-85217-512-2

Edwards

MOTTO:
God be our strength
(and)
When God willeth he will come
(and)
Truth conquers.

CREST:
An ibex
(and)
A demi-lion rampant.

NAME variations include:
Edward

Chapter one:

The origins of popular surnames

by George Forbes and Iain Gray

If you don't know where you came from, you won't know where you're going **is a frequently quoted observation and one that has a particular resonance today when there has been a marked upsurge in interest in genealogy, with increasing numbers of people curious to trace their family roots.**

Main sources for genealogical research include census returns and official records of births, marriages and deaths – and the key to unlocking the detail they contain is obviously a family surname, one that has been 'inherited' and passed from generation to generation.

No matter our station in life, we all have a surname – but it was not until about the middle of the fourteenth century that the practice of being identified by a particular surname became commonly established throughout the British Isles.

Previous to this, it was normal for a person to be identified through the use of only a forename.

But as population gradually increased and there were many more people with the same forename, surnames were adopted to distinguish one person, or community, from another.

Many common English surnames are patronymic in origin, meaning they stem from the forename of one's father – with 'Johnson,' for example, indicating 'son of John.'

It was the Normans, in the wake of their eleventh century conquest of Anglo-Saxon England, a pivotal moment in the nation's history, who first brought surnames into usage – although it was a gradual process.

For the Normans, these were names initially based on the title of their estates, local villages and chateaux in France to distinguish and identify these landholdings.

Such grand descriptions also helped enhance the prestige of these warlords and generally glorify their lofty positions high above the humble serfs slaving away below in the pecking order who had only single names, often with Biblical connotations as in Pierre and Jacques.

The only descriptive distinctions among the peasantry concerned their occupations, like 'Pierre the swineherd' or 'Jacques the ferryman.'

Roots of surnames that came into usage in England not only included Norman-French, but also Old French, Old Norse, Old English, Middle English, German, Latin, Greek, Hebrew and the Gaelic languages of the Celts.

The Normans themselves were originally Vikings, or 'Northmen', who raided, colonised and eventually settled down around the French coastline.

The had sailed up the Seine in their longboats in 900AD under their ferocious leader Rollo and ruled the roost in north eastern France before sailing over to conquer England in 1066 under Duke William of Normandy – better known to posterity as William the Conqueror, or King William I of England.

Granted lands in the newly-conquered England, some of their descendants later acquired territories in Wales, Scotland and Ireland – taking not only their own surnames, but also the practice of adopting a surname, with them.

But it was in England where Norman rule and custom first impacted, particularly in relation to the adoption of surnames.

This is reflected in the famous *Domesday Book*, a massive survey of much of England and Wales, ordered by William I, to determine who owned what, what it was worth and therefore how much they were liable to pay in taxes to the voracious Royal Exchequer.

Completed in 1086 and now held in the National Archives in Kew, London, 'Domesday' was an Old English word meaning 'Day of Judgement.'

This was because, in the words of one contemporary chronicler, "its decisions, like those of the Last Judgement, are unalterable."

It had been a requirement of all those English landholders – from the richest to the poorest – that they identify themselves for the purposes of the survey and for future reference by means of a surname.

This is why the *Domesday Book*, although written in Latin as was the practice for several centuries with both civic and ecclesiastical records, is an invaluable source for the early appearance of a wide range of English surnames.

Several of these names were coined in connection with occupations.

These include Baker and Smith, while Cooks, Chamberlains, Constables and Porters were to be found carrying out duties in large medieval households.

The church's influence can be found in names such as Bishop, Friar and Monk while the popular name of Bennett derives from the late fifth to mid-sixth century Saint Benedict, founder of the Benedictine order of monks.

The early medical profession is represented by Barber, while businessmen produced names that include Merchant and Sellers.

Down at the village watermill, the names that cropped up included Millar/Miller, Walker and Fuller, while other self-explanatory trades included Cooper, Tailor, Mason and Wright.

Even the scenery was utilised as in Moor, Hill, Wood and Forrest – while the hunt and the chase supplied names that include Hunter, Falconer, Fowler and Fox.

Colours are also a source of popular surnames, as in Black, Brown, Gray/Grey, Green and White, and would have denoted the colour of the clothing the person habitually wore or, apart from the obvious exception of 'Green', one's hair colouring or even complexion.

The surname Red developed into Reid, while

Blue was rare and no-one wanted to be associated with yellow.

Rather self-important individuals took surnames that include Goodman and Wiseman, while physical attributes crept into surnames such as Small and Little.

Many families proudly boast the heraldic device known as a Coat of Arms, as featured on our front cover.

The central motif of the Coat of Arms would originally have been what was borne on the shield of a warrior to distinguish himself from others on the battlefield.

Not featured on the Coat of Arms, but high-lighted on page three, is the family motto and related crest – with the latter frequently different from the central motif.

Adding further variety to the rich cultural heritage that is represented by surnames is the appearance in recent times in lists of the 100 most common names found in England of ones that include Khan, Patel and Singh – names that have proud roots in the vast sub-continent of India.

Echoes of a far distant past can still be found in our surnames and they can be borne with pride in commemoration of our forebears.

Chapter two:

Royal roots

**Although a surname found throughout the length
and breadth of the British Isles and much further
afield, 'Edwards' is primarily identified with Wales.**

Derived from the Old English 'eadward',
indicating 'prosperity guard' or 'prosperous guardian'
– with 'ead' denoting 'prosperity' and 'ward' meaning
'guard' – 'Edwards' developed as a surname from what
remains to this day the popular forename 'Edward.'

'Prosperity guard' may have referred to
someone entrusted with guarding a person's wealth
while 'prosperous guardian' could have been someone
with responsibility for the well-being of a minor, in
the role of 'guardian'.

As a forename, it was first popularised
through reverence for two separate Anglo-Saxon
monarchs – the tenth century Edward the Martyr and
the eleventh century Edward the Confessor.

Both kings were descended from those
Germanic tribes who invaded and settled in the south
and east of the island of Britain from about the early
fifth century.

Known as the Anglo-Saxons, they were composed of the Jutes, from the area of the Jutland Peninsula in modern Denmark, the Saxons from Lower Saxony, in modern Germany and the Angles from the Angeln area of Germany.

It was the Angles who gave the name 'Engla land', or 'Aengla land' – better known as 'England.'

They held sway in what became England from approximately 550 to 1066, with the main kingdoms those of Sussex, Wessex, Northumbria, Mercia, Kent, East Anglia and Essex.

Whoever controlled the most powerful of these kingdoms was tacitly recognised as overall 'king' – one of the most noted being Alfred the Great, King of Wessex from 871 to 899.

It was during his reign that the famous *Anglo-Saxon Chronicle* was compiled – an invaluable source of Anglo-Saxon history – while Alfred was designated in early documents as *Rex Anglorum Saxonum*, King of the English Saxons.

Born in about 962, the Edward who became known as Edward the Martyr was the eldest son of King Edgar, one of Alfred the Great's descendants.

On Edgar's death in 975, the young Edward was proclaimed king, but his right to the throne was contested by a group of powerful nobles who considered it in their interests to have his younger half-brother, Ethelred, assume the mantle of kingship.

With rival factions competing for influence and control over the two young boys, Edward was murdered under mysterious circumstances in Corfe Castle, Dorset, in 978.

Later interred with great ceremony in Shaftesbury Abbey, by which time it had emerged that his mother, the Queen Dowager, had been largely instrumental in his murder, Edward the Martyr is now recognised as a saint by the Roman Catholic Church, the Anglican Communion and the Eastern Orthodox Church.

Ethelred was duly crowned king following his half-brother's murder and, in view of how the inexperienced youth was suddenly thrust into kingship, he became better known to posterity as Ethelred the Unready.

He was the father of the monarch who became known as Edward the Confessor – also responsible, along with Edward the Martyr, for popularising the forename that later developed into the surname of Edwards.

Born in about 1003 and regarded as the last

Anglo-Saxon king of the Royal House of Wessex, the pious Edward ruled from 1042 until his death in January of 1066.

Canonised by Pope Alexander II, he was regarded as the national saint of England until 1350, when Edward III adopted Saint George as the nation's patron saint.

Following the death of Edward the Confessor, England had become a nation with several powerful competitors to the throne.

In what were extremely complex family, political and military machinations, the monarch was Harold II, who had succeeded to the throne following the death of Edward the Confessor.

But his right to the throne was contested by two powerful competitors – his brother-in-law King Harold Hardrada of Norway, in alliance with Tostig, Harold II's brother, and Duke William II of Normandy.

In what has become known as The Year of Three Battles, Hardrada invaded England and gained victory over the English king on September 20 at the battle of Fulford, in Yorkshire. Five days later, however, Harold II decisively defeated his brother-in-law and brother at the battle of Stamford Bridge.

But he had little time to celebrate his victory,

having to immediately march south from Yorkshire to encounter a mighty invasion force, led by Duke William of Normandy, that had landed at Hastings, in East Sussex.

Harold's battle-hardened but exhausted force confronted the Normans on October 14 in a battle subsequently depicted on the Bayeux tapestry – a 23ft. long strip of embroidered linen thought to have been commissioned eleven years after the event by the Norman Odo of Bayeux.

It was at the top of Senlac Hill that Harold drew up a strong defensive position, building a shield wall to repel Duke William's cavalry and infantry.

The Normans suffered heavy losses, but through a combination of the deadly skill of their archers and the ferocious determination of their cavalry they eventually won the day.

Anglo-Saxon morale had collapsed on the battlefield as word spread through the ranks that Harold had been killed – the Bayeux Tapestry depicting this as having happened when the English king was struck by an arrow to the head.

Amidst the carnage of the battlefield, it was difficult to identify Harold – the last of the Anglo-Saxon kings.

Some sources assert William ordered his body to be thrown into the sea, while others state it was secretly buried at Waltham Abbey.

What is known with certainty, however, is that William, in celebration of his great victory, founded Battle Abbey, near the site of the battle, ordering that the altar be sited on the spot where Harold was believed to have fallen.

William was declared King of England on December 25, and the complete subjugation of his Anglo-Saxon subjects followed.

Those Normans who had fought on his behalf were rewarded with the lands of Anglo-Saxons, many of whom sought exile abroad as mercenaries.

Within an astonishingly short space of time, Norman manners, customs and law were imposed on England – laying the basis for what subsequently became established 'English' custom and practice.

But beneath the surface, old Anglo-Saxon culture was not totally eradicated.

Some aspects were absorbed into those of the Normans, while faint echoes of the Anglo-Saxon past is still seen today in the form of popular surnames such as Edwards.

In Wales, where the Edwards name is particularly prevalent, some bearers claim a descent from a royal prince.

This is through the late twelfth century Einion Efell, Lord of Cynlleth, who in turn was a son of Madog ap Maredudd, the last prince of the Welsh kingdom of Powys, and who died in 1160.

Of Madog – whose name is sometimes also rendered as 'Madoc' – the ancient Welsh annals relate how:

While Madog lived there was no man
Dared ravage his fair borders
Yet nought of all he held
Esteemed he his save by God's might ...

In the seventeenth century, one bearer of the Edwards name who gained a particular infamy was Humphrey Edwards.

Born in 1582, he was one of the regicides – someone involved in the murder of a monarch – of Charles I.

The Catholic monarch had incurred the wrath of Parliament by his insistence on the 'divine right' of kings, and added to this was Parliament's fear of Catholic 'subversion' against the state and the king's stubborn refusal to grant demands for religious and constitutional concessions.

Matters came to a head with the outbreak of the Civil War in 1642, with Parliamentary forces, known as the New Model Army and commanded by Oliver Cromwell and Sir Thomas Fairfax, arrayed against the Royalist army of the king.

In what became an increasingly bloody and complex conflict, spreading to Scotland and Ireland and with rapidly shifting loyalties on both sides, the king was eventually captured and executed in January of 1649 on the orders of Parliament.

Both a lawyer and a prominent Parliamentarian, representing Shropshire, it was Humphrey Edwards who signed the ill-fated monarch's death warrant.

He died in 1658, two years before the Restoration of Charles II.

Chapter three:

Honours and distinction

From the seventeenth century English Civil War to the battlefields of later centuries, bearers of the Edwards name have gained distinction.

Born in 1885 in Lossiemouth, Morayshire, Alexander Edwards was a Scottish recipient during the Second World War of the Victoria Cross (VC), the highest award for valour in the face of enemy action for British and Commonwealth forces.

It was while serving with the 1/6th (Morayshire) Battalion, the Seaforth Highlanders, 51st Highland Division, that in September of 1917 during the battle of Passchendaele, in France, that he was instrumental – despite being wounded – in capturing and disabling an enemy machine-gun nest.

He was killed in action in March of the following year at Bapaume Wood, east of Arras, while his VC is now on display at the Regimental Museum of the Queen's Own Highlanders in Fort George, Inverness-shire.

Also during the First World War, Daniel

Edwards was a recipient of the Medal of Honor, America's highest award for military valour.

Born in 1897 in Moorville, Texas, he had been a Private First Class (PFC) with the 1st Division when, in July of 1918 near Soissons, France, he was single-handedly responsible for entering a trench and killing four of the enemy and capturing four others.

Also a recipient of the Distinguished Service Cross, he died in 1967.

In the skies above Europe during the Second World War, Air Commodore Sir Hughie Edwards was an Australian recipient of the VC.

Born in 1914, it was while serving as an RAF bomber pilot that in July of 1941 he led a daring low-level attack, codenamed Operation Wreckage, on the heavily defended German port of Bremen.

Later serving for a time as Governor of Western Australia, he died in 1982.

Also in the air, Glen Edwards was the Canadian-born U.S. Air Force pilot who distinguished himself during the Second World War and gained further distinction as a test pilot.

Born in 1918 in Medicine Hat, Alberta and moving with his parents when he was aged 13 to California, he was assigned during the war as a flight commander with the 86th Light Bombardment Squadron of the 47th Bombardment Group.

Serving from October of 1942 in the North African theatre of operations, his flight squadron was responsible for a number of missions that helped to earn it a Distinguished Unit Citation, while Edwards himself was awarded no fewer than four Distinguished Flying Crosses and six Air Medals.

Assigned as a test pilot to Bomber Test Operations in May of 1945, he became the principal pilot with a number of aircraft projects that included the jet-powered Convair XB-46 prototype bomber.

It was in June of 1948, while commander of the Muroc test base in California that he, along with co-pilot Daniel Forbes, was killed when the prototype Northrop YB-49 they were flying broke apart in the skies over the base – which was later named in Edwards's honour as Edwards Air Force Base.

An inductee of the International Aerospace Hall of Fame, Sir George Edwards was the British aircraft designer and industrialist who, in addition to his role of chief designer of the Vickers-Armstrong team that developed aircraft models including the Viscount and the Valiant, also had a role in the development of the supersonic aircraft Concorde.

Born in London in 1908 and for a time chairman of the British Aircraft Corporation (BAC), he died in 2003.

A leading British physicist, Sir Samuel Edwards was born in Swansea in 1928.

Involved since the 1950s in highly complex research that includes condensed matter physics, he served in the early 1970s as chairman of the Science Research Council and, from 1984 to 1995, as Cavendish Professor of Physics at Cambridge University.

Knighted in 1975 for his services to science, his many other awards include the Royal Medal of the Royal Society and the Boltzmann Medal of the International Union of Pure and Applied Physics.

One bearer of the proud name of Edwards who has left behind an enduring legacy was the British physiologist Sir Robert Edwards who, along with the surgeon Patrick Steptoe, successfully pioneered conception through in-vitro fertilisation (IVF).

This led, in July of 1978, to the birth of Louise Brown – the world's first IVF, or 'test-tube', baby. Since her birth, more than four million children worldwide have been born through the technique.

Born in Manchester in 1925, it was in 1960, after having studied at the Institute of Animal Genetics at Edinburgh University and other academic institutions, that he started to study human fertilisation.

In 1968, after achieving fertilisation of a human egg in the laboratory, he began his collaboration with Patrick Steptoe – and it was through their efforts that Louise Brown was able to be born ten years later in Oldham General Hospital.

The technique has provoked controversy on religious and ethical grounds, but Edwards, who died in April of 2013, 25 years after the death of Steptoe, became the recipient of many honours and awards.

Awarded the 2010 Nobel Prize in Physiology or Medicine and knighted a year later for services to human reproductive biology, he was also ranked in his lifetime at No. 26 in a *Daily Telegraph* list of 100 greatest living geniuses.

Chapter four:

On the world stage

Known for his 'trademark' handlebar moustache, James O'Neill Edwards was the English comedy scriptwriter and actor on both radio and television better known as Jimmy Edwards.

Born in 1920 in Barnes, London, the son of a professor of mathematics, it was while serving in the RAF during the Second World War that he was shot down over Arnhem.

This resulted in facial injuries that required plastic surgery – and it was to disguise the traces of an operation to his upper lip that he grew his moustache.

A recipient of the Distinguished Flying Cross (DFC), he first came to attention as an entertainer as the character Pa Glum in the radio series *Take It From Here*, co-starring with Dick Bentley, and later as 'Professor' James Edwards in the television comedy series *Whack-O!*

Film credits include the 1948 *Trouble in the Air* and the 1969 *Rhubarb*, while before his death in 1988 he also starred in a number of short films written by fellow comedian Eric Sykes, including the 1967 *The Plank*.

First appearing on radio in the 1930s in *The Adventures of Sonny and Buddy*, America's first radio series to be nationally syndicated, **Sam Edwards** was the actor born in 1915 in Macon, Georgia.

His many television credits include *Gunsmoke*, *Laramie*, *Little House on the Prairie* and *The Dukes of Hazzard*, while big screen credits include the 1949 *Twelve O'Clock High* and the 1981 *The Postman Always Rings Twice*.

Also the voice of the adult Thumper in the 1942 animated film classic *Bambi*, he died in 2004.

Born in London in 1971, **Jeremy Edwards** is the actor and television presenter best known for his roles in popular British television shows that include the medical drama *Holby City* and the soap *Hollyoaks*.

Born in 1922 in Tulsa, Oklahoma, William Blake Crump was the prolific American film director, producer and screenwriter better known as **Blake Edwards**.

Responsible for the highly successful *Pink Panther* series of films, starring Peter Sellers, his other notable works include the 1959 *Operation Petticoat*, the 1961 *Breakfast at Tiffany's* and the 1969 *Darling Lili* – which starred Julie Andrews, his second wife.

The recipient of an Honorary Academy Award, he died in 2010.

In the contemporary world of the media, **Huw Edwards** is the award-winning Welsh journalist, television presenter and newsreader born in 1961 in Bridgend, Glamorgan.

Joining the BBC in 1984 after obtaining a degree in French from University College, Cardiff, and working for a time with the radio station Swansea Sound, he has since gone on to present flagship BBC television programmes that include *News at Ten*.

He is the son of the late Welsh academic and historian **Hywel Teifi Edwards**, born in 1934. A noted author in the Welsh language and also a prominent Welsh nationalist, he died in 2010.

From Welsh shores to Irish shores, **Robert Dudley Edwards** was the distinguished historian born in Dublin in 1909.

Gaining a first class degree in history from University College, Dublin, in 1929, followed two years later with a first class master's degree, he was professor of modern Irish history at the college from 1944 until his retirement in 1979.

Author of works that include his 1935 *Church and State in Tudor Ireland* and the 1972 *A New History of Ireland*, he died in 1988.

He was the father of the historian **Owen Dudley Edwards**, born in Dublin in 1938.

Reader in Commonwealth and American History at Edinburgh University and general editor of the *Oxford Sherlock Holmes* series of books, he is also the author of works that include his 1970 *The Sins of our Fathers*, the 1977 *P.G. Wodehouse: A Critical and Historical Essay* and, from 2007, *British Children's Fiction in the Second World War*.

He is the brother of the historian, novelist, journalist and broadcaster **Ruth Dudley Edwards**, born in Dublin in 1944.

In addition to her work as a historian and in the media, she has also held posts that include chairwoman of the British Association for Irish Studies and, since 2009, director of the Centre for Social Cohesion.

Not only a novelist but also an artist, **Graham Edwards** is the English author of fantasy and crime novels born in Somerset in 1965. The illustrator of some of his own novels, he is particularly known for his best-selling *The Ultimate Dragon* trilogy and the *Stone* trilogy.

Bearers of the Edwards name have also excelled in the highly competitive world of sport.

At the time of writing the holder since 1995 of the world record in the triple jump, **Jonathan Edwards** is the British former athlete who won the gold medal in the event at the 2000 Olympics in Sydney.

It was at the World Championship five years previous to this that he set the world record in the event, while his many other accomplishments include winning the gold medal at the 2002 Commonwealth Games.

Born in Windsor in 1966 and a recipient of the CBE and named BBC Sports Personality of the Year in 1995, he is now a presenter and commentator on athletics for the BBC.

Also in athletics, **Clancy Edwards** is the American former sprinter who won the 200-metres event at the 1977 World Championship in Dusseldorf.

Born in 1955, he was also ranked in 1978 at No. 2 in the world in the 100-metres sprint discipline.

From the athletics track to the motorcycle racing circuit, **Colin Edwards**, born in 1974 in

Houston, Texas, is the rider who was World Superbike Champion in both 2000 and 2002.

On the golf course, **David Edwards**, born in 1956 in Neosho, Missouri, is the American golfer who played on the PGA (Professional Golfers Association) Tour from 1979 to 2005; later a player on the Champions Tour, he is the younger brother of the former PGA professional **Danny Edwards**, who was born in 1951.

In the rough and tumble that is the game of rugby union, **Shaun Edwards** is the coach and former player born in 1966 in Wigan, Lancashire.

The recipient of an OBE, he played for England from 1995 to 1996 and, in 2008, was appointed a coach for the Welsh national team.

On the cricket pitch, **Charlotte Edwards**, born in 1979 in Huntingdon, Cambridgeshire is the cricketer who was appointed captain of England's women team in 2006; a player of county cricket for Kent, she was named the ICC (International Cricket Council) Women's Cricketer of the Year for 2008.

On the fields of European football, **Dave Edwards** is the English-born midfielder who, through his grand-parentage, qualified to play for the Welsh national team.

Born in 1986 in Shrewsbury, he first started playing for Wales in 2007, while clubs he has played for include Shrewsbury Town, Luton Town and Wolverhampton Wanderers.

Born in 1936 in Dudley, Warwickshire, **Duncan Edwards** was the Manchester United footballer who was one of the victims of the Munich air disaster in February of 1958.

One of the 'Busby Babes', the young Manchester United team managed by Matt Busby, the talented wing-half was one of the eight players and fourteen other passengers and crew who died when their aircraft crashed on take-off after a refuelling stop in Munich.

They had been returning from a game against Red Star Belgrade.

Edwards initially survived the crash, but died in hospital twenty days later from his injuries.

A street in his hometown of Dudley is named in his honour, while he is also portrayed by the actor Sam Claflin in the 2011 British television film *United*, based on the Munich disaster.

In the world of music, **David "Honeyboy" Edwards** was the famous Delta blues guitarist born in 1915 in Shaw, Mississippi.

The last of the original Delta blues guitarists – with 'Delta' indicating their roots in the American South – his many recordings include *Wind Howlin Blues* and his 1942 *Army Blues*.

An inductee of the Blues Hall of Fame and a recipient of a National Heritage Fellowship Award from America's National Endowment for the Arts, he died in 2011.

Born in Germany in 1879 and immigrating to the United States with his family when he was aged seven, Gus Simon was the songwriter and theatrical producer better known as **Gus Edwards**.

As a songwriter, it was in collaboration with others that he penned songs that include *By the Light of the Silvery Moon* and *In My Merry Oldsmobile*, while as a theatrical agent he discovered and promoted famous acts that include the Marx Brothers.

An inductee of the Songwriters Hall of Fame, he died in 1945, while he was also the brother of **Leo Edwards**, the Broadway composer born in 1886; with writing credits that include compositions for *The Wizard of Oz*, he died in 1978.

In contemporary music, **Kathleen Edwards**, born in 1978 in Ottawa, is the best-selling Canadian singer and songwriter whose album credits include her debut 2003 *Failer*, the 2005 *Back to Me* and, from 2012, *Voyageur*.

One musician with a particularly unusual claim to enduring celebrity status was **Richard James Edwards**, also known as Richard James, who disappeared under mysterious circumstances.

Born in 1967 in Caerphilly, he was the rhythm guitarist and lyricist for the best-selling Welsh alternative rock band Manic Street Preachers.

It was in February of 1995 that he disappeared, after having withdrawn money from his bank account over a successive period of days.

His car was eventually located by police in a service station near the Severn Bridge – and it is assumed the musician, who suffered from drug and alcohol problems, may have taken his life by jumping from the bridge.

But his body has never been found, and it was not until November of 2008 that he was legally presumed dead.

His mysterious disappearance has since fuelled a number of theories and claims – including that he had been spotted living in a hippy commune in Goa, India.